THE BUSHCRAFT HANDBOOKS

BUSH CAMPCRAFT

Illustrations by the Author

Richard H. Graves

The Bushcraft Handbooks
Bush Campcraft

This Edition Copyright © 2013 by Palmer River Publishing

Cover, Graphics and Layout by: Palmer River Publishing

All rights reserved. No part of this book may be reproduced in any form by any electronic or mechanical means including photocopying, recording, or information storage and retrieval without permission in writing from the author.

ISBN-13: 978-1484812761
ISBN-10: 148481276X

About The Author

The author of "The Bushcraft Handbooks", Richard Graves, is a member of the Irish literary family of that name. A veteran of the Great War campaigns in the Dardenelles and the Western Front, the author became passionate about the bush at an early age. As an enthusiastic bushwalker, skier and pioneer of white-water canoeing, he foresaw how a knowledge of bushcraft could save lives in the Second World War. To achieve this end, he initiated and led the Australian Jungle Rescue Detachment, assigned to the Far East American Air Force. This detachment of 60 specially selected A.I.F. soldiers successfully effected more than 300 rescue missions, most of which were in enemy-held territory in New Guinea, without failure of a mission or loss of a man.

An essential preliminary for rescue was survival, and it was for this purpose that the notes for these books were written. These notes were later revised and prepared for a School in Bushcraft which has been operating for several years and continues to provide valuable instruction to Servicemen embarking overseas on active service in Korea and Malaya.

Bushcraft

As far as is known, "The Bushcraft Handbooks" are unique. There is nothing quite like them, nor is any collection of published bushcraft knowledge as comprehensive.

The term "Bushcraft" is used because "woodcraft" commonly means either knowledge of local fauna and flora or else is associated with the blood-sports of hunting and shooting. "The Bushcraft Handbooks" include a volume on traps and snares, but these are purposely-designed to be completely ineffective for native animals which are insect enters or grazers. These traps have been included because they would only be effective in catching predatory animals such as cats and dogs which have taken to the bush, and other "pest" creatures such as feral swine or goat.

"Bushcraft" describes the activity of how to make use of natural materials found locally in any area. It includes many of the skills used by primitive man, and to these are added "white man" skills necessary for survival, such as time and direction, and the provision of modern "white man" comforts as illustrated in the volume on bush campcraft.

The practice of bushcraft develops in an individual a remarkable ability to adapt quickly to a changing environment. Because this is so, the activity is a valuable counter to the over-specialisation so prevalent in today's society, and is particularly significant in youth training and character-moulding work.

INTRODUCTION to the BUSHCRAFT HANDBOOKS

THE PRACTICE OF BUSHCRAFT shows many unexpected results. The five senses are sharpened, and consequently the joy of being alive is greater. The individual's ability to adapt and improvise is developed to a remarkable degree. This in turn leads to increased self-confidence.

Self-confidence, and the ability to adapt to a changing environment and to overcome difficulties, is followed by a rapid improvement in the individual's daily work. This in turn leads to advancement and promotion.

Bushcraft, by developing adaptability, provides a broadening influence, a necessary counter to offset the narrowing influence of modern specialisation.

For this work of bushcraft all that is needed is a sharp cutting implement: knife, axe or machete. The last is the most useful. For the work, dead materials are most suitable. The practice of bushcraft conserves, and does not destroy, wild life.

R.H.G.
April, 1952

CONTENTS

About The Author	iii
Bushcraft	iii
INTRODUCTION to the BUSHCRAFT HANDBOOKS	v
BUSH CAMPCRAFT	1
Campcraft	2
Stakes and Pegs	2
Forks	3
Hooks	4
Driving Stakes	4
Camp Kitchens	5
Fireplaces	5
Billy Hooks and Fire Tongs	9
Woodshed	11
Firewood and Fire in the Rain	11
Boiling and Baking Without Utensils	14
Camp Furniture	19
Tables	19
Camp Chairs	23
Camp Seat	26
Camp Beds	27
Camp Bed Off the Ground	28
Camp Bed Using a Couple of Bags	29
Stick Hammock	30
Camp Loom	31
To Weave on a Camp Loom	32
Camp Mattress of Stick Hammock	32
Weaving a Camp Hammock	33
Bush Ladder	34
Single Rope Ladder	34
Swinging Shelter	35
Slush Lamp	36
A Candle Holder From a Bottle	37
Noggin	38
Clothes Pegs	38
Camp Broom	39

Bush Hoe 39
Bush Sled 40
Camp Larder 40
Camp Coat Hanger 42
Camp Pack Frame 42

Camp Sun Clock 43
To Find the Sun's Position North or
South of the Equator 45

BUSH CAMPCRAFT

With the only tool a machete or a sharp knife, it is practical and easy to set up a camp in comfort. Everything one needs for bed, table, seats and chairs, cooking, and even lighting is usually available in the area immediately around the camp.

A small amount of knowledge is needed and some of this is given in this book.

Campcraft, like all the other skills in bushcraft develops the powers of observation to a remarkable degree, and with this the ability to adapt or improvise.

It is applicable by all who camp, regardless of whether the camping is a once-a-year venture with a car and auto tent, or a weekend adventure with a pack on one's back.

There need be no discomfort for anyone in camping if they have knowledge of how to set up a camp in comfort.

A properly made camp bed can be as restful as a sprung mattress, and no food is more flavoursome than when cooked in the out-of-doors.

If the camper does not know how to camp in comfort there will be times during heavy rain when wood appears too wet to take fire, or when the wind is so high that the heat of the fire is blown under and away from the water in the billy the camper is trying to boil, or when ants or bush rats find the food supply.

This book shows many things you can do to make

your camping more comfortable, and considerably safer.

Campcraft

Campcraft without equipment is totally different from campcraft with equipment ... and in some ways, "doing without" can be more fun. This volume of "The Bushcraft Handbooks" shows things that you can make and do in camp when you have no equipment except a cutting tool. Some items will be new to even the most experienced camper, and there will be much that is of value to the Boy Scout and the Serviceman.

Camping without equipment calls for a really sharp tool, and a good deal of common sense. A good machete is probably the most useful of all tools for bush work. Mostly you will want sticks, either for pegs or stakes, or forks or hooks, and these generally can be cut from windblown branches close to the site of your camp.

It is always preferable to use dead timber rather than growing wood. By using dead (but not rotten) wood you are clearing the forest floor of debris, and by avoiding cutting green wood you are helping to conserve the forests.

Stakes and Pegs

Even a simple item like a stake or a peg must be cut properly, and if it is to be driven into the ground it must have the head bevelled and the toe properly pointed.

THIS IS THE RIGHT WAY

This stake will drive cleanly into the ground. It will not split when being driven because the head is properly bevelled.

THESE ARE WRONG

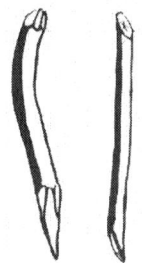

Both these stakes will be a failure. One will not drive because it has a bend, and this deflects the blow. The other will either split at the head, or drive crooked, because the toe is cut at an angle.

Forks

Generally the correct sort of fork to select is one with a perfectly straight drive from the head to the toe, and with the forked stick coming off at an angle. A fork which is to be driven into the ground must have the head bevelled and the toe pointed.

THIS FORK IS CORRECT   THESE FORKS ARE WRONG

 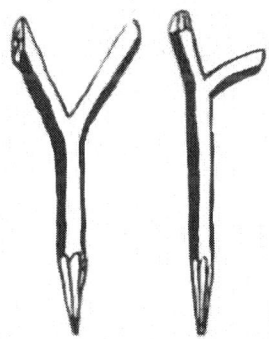

There is a perfectly straight drive from the bevelled head right through to the toe. This fork will drive into the ground and stand securely.

These forks cannot be driven. Left: If you try to hit one of the forks, the blow will be deflected by the angle. If you try to hit in the crotch, the fork will split. Right: Because the main stick is not straight, this fork will not go into the ground.

Most beginners think that the wrong way will work out all right . . . everyone does . . . the first time; then you learn that it pays to spend five minutes finding the right shaped stake or fork, rather than trying-to make do with a poorly selected stick.

Hooks

Unless hooks are to be driven into the ground, less care is required for their selection.

THIS HOOK WILL DO THE JOB

AND SO WILL THIS

After you have selected the stake, fork or hook, and before you trim it, make sure that the wood, though dead, is not rotten. The inner wood must be sound.

Driving Stakes

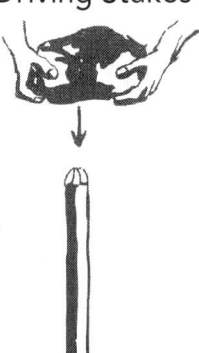

Stakes can be driven into the ground either by using the back of an axe for a maul, or if an axe is not available, a large stone, held in the two hands, and "pulled" down to the head of the stake, will drive quite effectively. When using a stone, if it is flat, use the edge rather than the flat. The edge will put more weight behind the drive, and there will be less chance of the stone breaking in two with the force of the blow. If stones of a convenient size are not available, a club with one flat face can be quickly fashioned with a tomahawk or heavy knife, and this will serve effectively.

Camp Kitchens

The camp kitchen should be sited so that the breeze will not blow the smoke into the cook's face. This is quite easy when you know which direction the winds blow, both in the morning and the evening. The morning breeze (anabatic, if you want to be technical) blows up the valley, because the warm air of the valley floor rises; and the evening breeze (catabatic) blows down the valley. Therefore set your kitchen so that the cook will face neither up valley nor down valley from the fire, but sideways. Thus the smoke will blow past him, and he can cook in comfort.

The kitchen should be sited on a slight rise so that during rain it will not be flooded. The fireplace, in badly drained ground, should be built up a few inches above ground level. Select the place for your fire, and build the kitchen round it.

Fireplaces

If stones are available, build a wall to enclose the fire. This wall should be about nine or ten inches high, and the opening should be parallel to the valley. Do not take stones from a watercourse. They will explode in the fire.

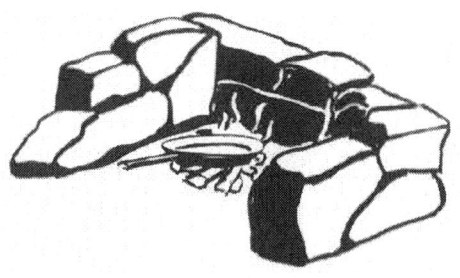

You will want a means of suspending your billies, and the most simple is a stick across the end walls.

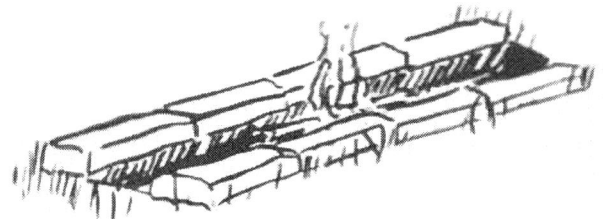

A trench fireplace is an efficient cooking place, but only suitable in clayey soil and if there is no likelihood of flooding.

A third method is a single stick, lying over one of the end stones, and with its farther end held down either under a hooked stake or by a heavy stone.

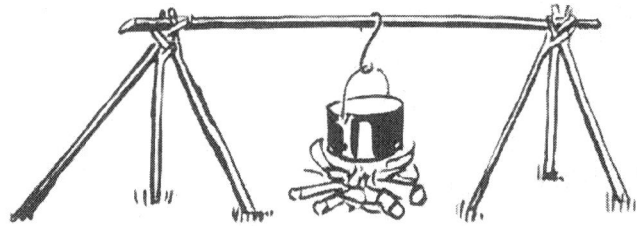

Two simply erected tripods of interlocking forked sticks at either end, with a cross stick, is another method of suspending your billies over the fire. This latter has the advantage that, by changing the base of the tripods, the height of the billy above the flames can be varied.

Another method to suspend your billies is by an overhead stick supported by two forked stakes driven into the ground at either end of the stone wall.

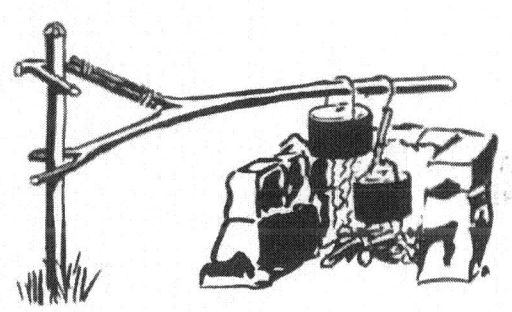

The best method of all, in a permanent camp, calls for a single straight stake driven into the ground at one side of the fireplace, and from this single stake a swinging gantry is hung. The height of the gantry on the upright stake can be adjusted to any height above the fire. It will swing free of the flames, and the billies can be taken off without burning your fingers. Although it may take five minutes to make, it will save burnt fingers and spilt or spoilt meals.

In flooded country, or in a marsh or swamp land, it may be impossible to find a spot of dry land on which to light a fire. One way to overcome this is to build a raised platform with its floor a few inches above the water level. The sticks which make the base of the platform are covered with a thick layer of mud. On this you can light your fire and cook your meal.

In the absence of stones, and where green wood of no value (such as sucker growth) is plentiful, a reflector fireplace may commend itself to you, particularly if the location is windy. The reflector should be on the windward side of the fire, so that the wind, passing over it, draws the flames up to the top of the reflector and then across.

When you want to boil a billy quickly in an open space in a very high wind, the flames will be blown away if, the billy is suspended. Bushmen have a trick that is worth using under such conditions. Place the billy on the ground, and build the fire to windward and on both sides of the billy. The wind will blow the hot flames around the sides and your billy will soon boil.

Billy Hooks and Fire Tongs

All of these methods of suspending billies over a fire are improved with the use of billy hooks, and these can be easily made by cutting a few hooked sticks about half an inch in diameter, and varying in length from, say, six to ten inches. At the end farthest from the hook, a single deep nick is cut into the wood, so that the direction of the cut is away from the hook. The wire handle of the billy will sit safely in this nick and the billy stick from which the billy hooks hang will be sufficiently far from the flames so that there will be little chance of it being burnt through. It is preferable to suspend the billy on the side opposite to the hook.

It is worth while making a couple of adjustable wire billy hooks if you go camping frequently. The advantages of being able to have one billy high above the flames so that it can simmer gently, and another right down over the fire to boil quickly, is apparent.

The adjustable billy hook is held at whatever height you set it by the link which locks it securely.

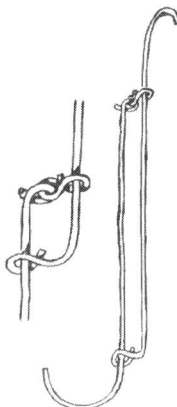

Adjustable wire billy hook

In addition to your billy stick and billy hooks, you would be well advised to make a pair of fire tongs. They will take only a few minutes, but may save a badly burnt hand.

Another improvised pair of fire tongs uses a narrow but long fork, and a single stick through its crutch.

Woodshed

And finally, you will want to be prepared against a spell of wet weather, and so you'll need a small woodshed. Only then will there be a supply of dry kindling and wood after heavy rain.

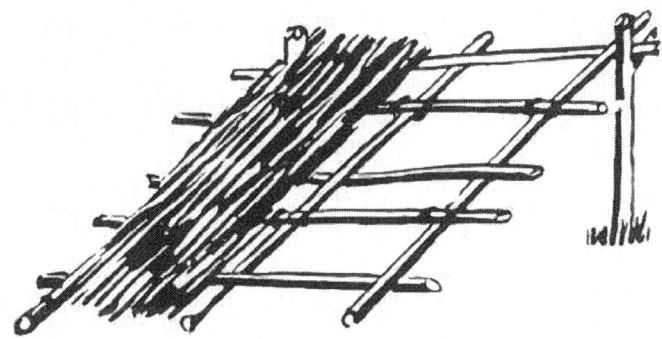

The ground dimensions of your woodshed should be at least three feet by four, and about three feet high at the front. It should be to windward of your fireplace, so that windblown sparks will not fall on dry bark or other tinder.

Firewood and Fire in the Rain

Firewood gathered from the ground after rain will be damp and unsuitable for a good fire. This applies to winter conditions and in rain forest, except after a long drought. It is far wiser, if you want a good fire, to pull down dead branches standing on trees for your firewood store. This wood is always reasonably dry.

When cutting thick sticks into short lengths, an easy way is to make deep cuts, opposite each other, on either side of the stick, and then, taking the stick, bring it down sharply on to a convenient log or rock, with the cut area at the point of impact. One sharp blow will generally break the wood, and you will save yourself the work of cutting right through the wood.

Always cut and store an ample supply of firewood in your woodshed in a standing camp. You never know when you may get a spell of rainy weather. Lighting a fire with wood soaked after a heavy night's rain is not easy, even for the expert, and you'll appreciate your store of dry wood.

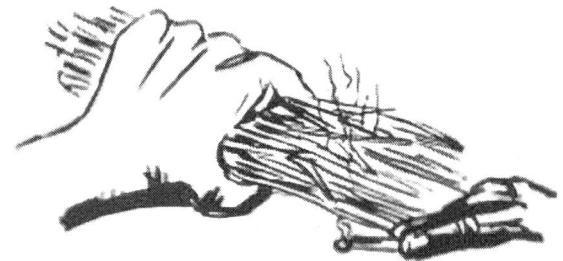

After rain or heavy dew, you can start a fire by picking a big handful of thin dead twigs from nearby bushes. Hold these in your hand and apply the match flame to the end of the twigs. Keep twisting and turning until the whole handful is well alight.

If the twigs are too wet you may have to make a few "fuzz" sticks. Select dead wood standing from a shrub and break into sticks about f-inch thick and ten inches long. Cut away the wet outer wood, and trim the dry wood down in feathers. Three or four of these "fuzz" sticks will start your fire.

If it is raining heavily at the time, start your fire in your tent, and carry the twigs or "fuzz" sticks when well alight to the fireplace in your billy. Shield the early fire from the rain with your body. A slush lamp will always start a fire, even with wet twigs.

The bandage in your first-aid kit previously soaked in kerosene will give you a starter for a fire. The kerosene will not affect the usefulness of the bandage.

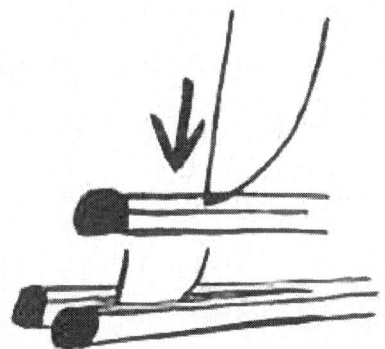

You can make one match light two fires by splitting the match. Hold the point of a sharp knife just below the head of the match and press down sharply. When using a split match to light a fire prime the twigs with dry grass or teased dry bark fibre.

Boiling and Baking Without Utensils

In emergency you may want to boil water, or cook food in boiling water, and you have no billy or utensil of any kind. This difficulty can be overcome by scooping a shallow hole in the ground and lining it with your groundsheet, some newspaper, a shirt, or any material which will hold the water. Build a quick fire of small sticks in which to heat twenty or thirty stones each two or three inches in diameter. Be very careful not to take these stones from a creek bed. Such stones may explode in the fire and injure you.

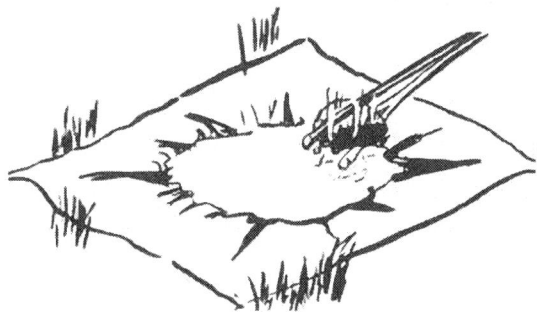

Fill the shallow hole with water, and when the stones are nearly red hot, which will take at least ten minutes, lift them one at a time from the fire with a pair of fire tongs and put gently into the water in the hole. The hot stones will not burn the paper or cloth, and five or six stones will bring a couple of quarts of water to boiling point in a matter of two or three minutes. Boiling temperature can be maintained for an indefinite period by putting in the other stones singly. Remove the cold stones when you put the hot ones in.

BARK DISH OR COOLAMIN

One method of improvising a cooking utensil is to make a bark dish, or Aboriginal "Coolamin".

A flat piece of bark, of a species which will not split easily (the bark of many trees has this quality; one is the ficus family, or "fig trees"; test first by stripping a small piece of bark from one of the branches), is softened in the hands, and then the two ends are folded as in the illustration and pinned with a thin, sharpened peg or tied to hold them in position.

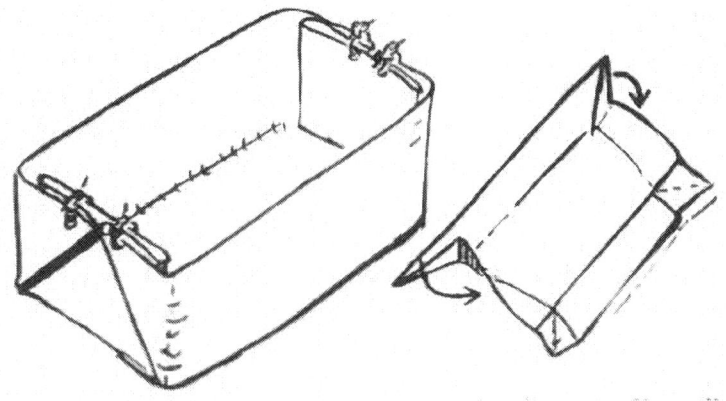

Coolamin made from folded green bark

A coolamin can be used for all sorts of cooking with hot stones.

It is necessary to use the bark of green trees for a coolamin. If the sap is coloured, particularly if it is white or whitish and you can't be sure it is "latex" or "rubber", be extremely careful not to get it in your eyes. Many saps can "burn" your skin, or blind you temporarily.

Meat can be grilled by using a forked stick with the fork ends sharpened. Alternatively, you can place a flat stone in the fire and get it nearly red hot. This hot flat stone should be removed from the fire and dusted clean. Place the meat to be cooked on it, and the meat will grill perfectly.

Baking can be done by making a stone oven, in which you light the fire and, when the stones are "sizzling" hot, draw the fire out of the oven, and place your scone or meat in the heated cavity. It will cook perfectly, and cannot burn, because the temperature is falling all the time.

An oil drum or large tin, if available, can be made into a good oven. Coat it thickly with several inches of clay. Build your fire either in the drum or tin, which is used like the stone oven, or alternatively, set the tin over a trench fireplace, and build one fire in the trench and another on top of the tin.

Another ready-made oven is to fire a hollow log or old stump. When the hollow is alight, place your cooking (covered on top and underneath) inside. You will have to watch all the time your food is cooking, because the fire may be too fierce and burn the baking. If the fire gets too fierce, damp it off with splashes of water.

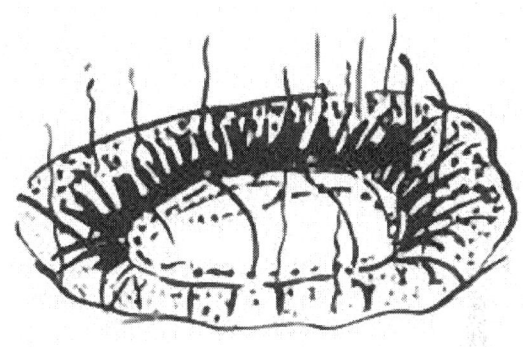

The best baking is done by wrapping the food in either a coating of clay or damp paper, and then burying it in the hot dust beneath your camp fire. Food can be left for six to eight hours without spoiling if the fire in not built up. The food will not overcook and you can rely on it being tender. This is one of the best ways to cook freshly-killed meat, which would otherwise be tough. When cooking fish and game by this method, it is not necessary to pluck, skin or "draw" the carcase. The intestines will shrivel up, and the outer skin, whether fur or feathers, will peel off when you unwrap the clay or paper.

A variation of this method of "primitive" cooking is to dig a hole which is lined with stones. This hole is "fired" with a quick fire so that the stones are thoroughly heated. When the fire has died down and there is only hot white ash left, the food, wrapped as before, is placed on the heated stones, and the whole covered over with the dirt removed in the digging of the hole. In this, as in the previous method of cooking, the food will not spoil or be burnt, and can be left for six to eight hours.

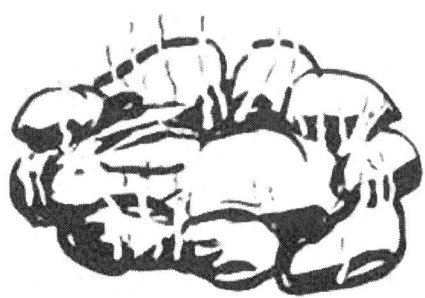

The cooking methods outlined are adaptable to the needs of the moment. For instance, it would be waste of time to build a stone fireplace on which to cook a single meal when on a walking tour. It would be far easier to select a suitably sheltered position in the lee of an earthy bank or rock. On the other hand, in a standing camp, time is well spent in making a good fireplace, secure against wind and bad weather. It is assumed that the reader has sufficient common sense to use the cooking method and fireplace best suited to his needs and to clear trash away from the neighbourhood of the fire, also never to leave a fire burning in a vacant camp.

An egg can be baked by placing it in the hot ashes of your fire. But first you must pierce the shell and inside skin to allow the steam to escape. The egg will blow up if this is not done.

Water which is very muddy, dirty or stagnant can be clarified and sterilised and made quite safe for drinking by filtering and boiling with hot stones. A good filter is made from a pair of drill trousers with one leg turned inside out and put inside the other leg. The cuff is tied, and the upper part held open by three stakes driven well into the ground. Fill with the dirty water, and then drop in the hot stones. The water will filter through, and must be caught either in a billy or bark dish and poured back until the dirt has been filtered out and the water is boiling.

Camp Furniture

Tables

A camp table and seats are worth making if there are five or six people in a standing camp, even if only for a few days. The best pattern of camp table is one which also carries the seats, and which will not become unbalanced or unsteady, even though several people sit on one side.

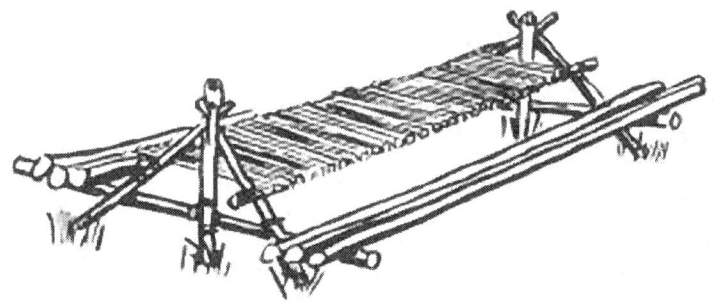

This is about the best style of camp table you construct. When you make it do not use green wood, but search through the bush and you will find dead timber, which is lighter in weight and quite strong, for forks and poles.

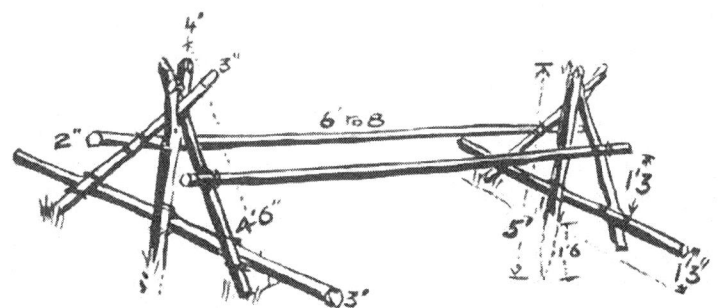

Showing the framework with table top poles and seat poles

For the framework select two forked stakes at least three inches thick and four to five feet long. The length depends upon the soil, and how far you will have to drive the stakes into the ground to make them quite secure. The lower end of each stake is sharpened and the head bevelled. The first stake should be driven well into the earth, so that the lowest part of the crotch of the fork is three feet above the ground. The prong of the fork should be pointing out from the length of the table. When this stake is set, measure off the length you want your table, say, from four to seven feet, and drive in the other stake with its prong also pointing outwards-that is, away from the first stake. This stake must also be driven the same depth into the ground as the first stake. Cut four strong straight stakes, four feet six to five feet in length, and at least two and a half inches thick. Place these with one end in the crotch of the forks, and at right angles to the line of the forked stakes. Note where the sticks cross each other in the forks, and scarf out cuts in each, so that the two will nest together in the crotch. These side poles carry the table poles and the seat poles, so they must "seat" securely in the forks.

On to these side poles, and about two feet above ground level, two strong poles, two inches thick, are securely lashed. These poles are for the table, and later straight sticks are laced side by side across these poles for the actual table top.

Fifteen inches above ground level, two very strong poles, three inches thick and seven or eight feet in length, are lashed. These lashings must be very tight to make these two poles secure to the two side poles and also to the forked stakes you first drove into the ground. These poles serve both as a bracing to carry the seat.

Your table is now ready for finishing. Cut short, straight sticks for the top. You will need eight sticks for every foot in length of table top. The method of lacing these to the table top poles is shown in the sketch below.

The seat-sticks—at least three to four inches thick—are cut a foot longer than the length of the table. You will need at least three of these seat-sticks for each side. They are not lashed to the cross poles, but allowed to lie on them, so that the distance of the seat from the table can be adjusted by either pushing the sticks back or pulling them in.

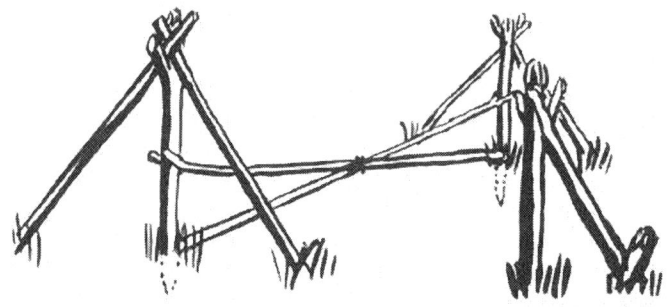

Sketch showing how to brace your table if the ground is soft or sandy

If the ground is soft, or loose sand, your table will require bracing, and this can be done simply by two diagonal braces from the table level of each of the forked stakes to the foot of the other. Where the bracings cross, they should be lashed. An alternative is to cut two five-foot forks and brace with these so that they "jam" below the forks of the stakes in the ground. Their own butts must be firmly seated on the ground and held from slipping; by a stout peg driven well in the ground.

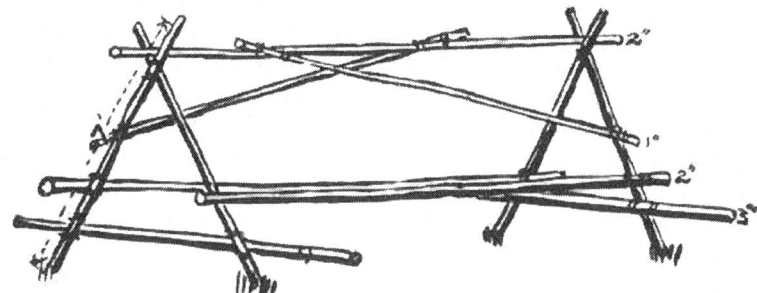

This type of structure is recommended for a portable table. When securely lashed the whole table is extremely strong. A fly thrown over the top bar can be used to give shade.

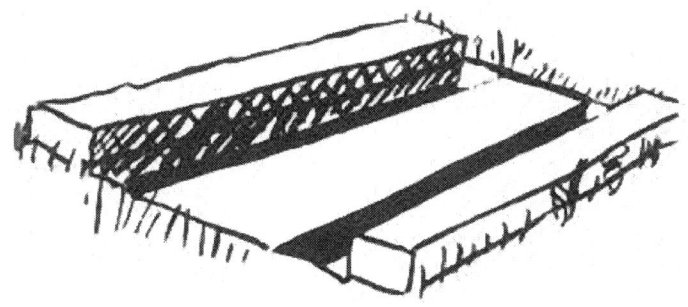

Another type of camp table, suitable for dry country, is to simply dig two trenches, two or three feet apart on their inside edges, and at least ten to twelve inches deep. This is only suitable when the earth is clayey or firm enough to be dug in clean sods. Sods are used to give height to the seat. When digging such a table, remember to replace the sods when you leave the camp site.

When using an earth table it is advisable to weave a couple of grass mats to lay over the seat. These will keep your clothes clean, and only take a few minutes to make on a camp loom.

Camp Chairs

A comfortable camp chair can be made in ten or fifteen minutes and will give you hours and hours of comfort. Select two stout forked sticks, four feet long and three inches thick. The forks must be at a wide angle, and cut with the straighter of the two prongs about nine to ten inches long, and the other wide angled prong about twelve to fifteen inches. Cut another stout forked stick about four feet in length, and leave the prongs of this sufficiently long to hold the two sticks you have previously cut.

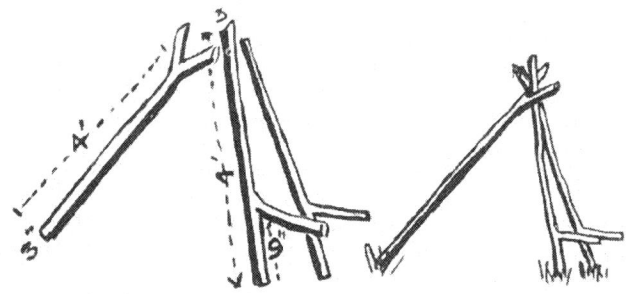

Showing the three main sticks required for a camp chair

    Across the seat portion of the chair, lash straight sticks about an inch thick, and continue these up the back of the chair. On the seat portion they must be close together, but on the back they can be spaced two or three inches apart.

Showing the framework of a chair using hooked sticks

    There may be difficulty in finding two sticks with wide angled prongs, in which case you can make your chair by using two hooked stakes. The crotch of the hook should be about eight inches above the end of the stick, and the sticks themselves should be about three feet six inches long.

Two side poles, each about five feet long, are laid one each through the hooked portion of the sticks, which have their upper ends lashed together. These two poles are lashed together behind the chair, and a forked pole, leading from the upper end where the hooked stakes are lashed, comes back to these two side poles and is lashed again. This gives you the framework for your chair.

Occasionally you will find a pair of twisty sticks which, lying on the ground, will look like this—

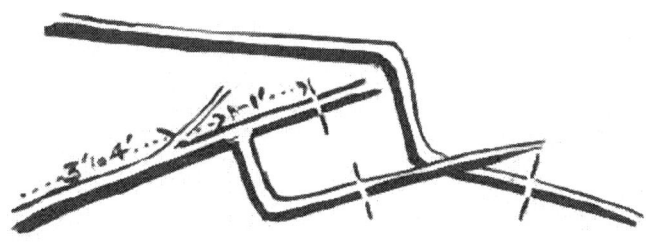

...but, if you are quick to see the opportunity they present, you will convert them into a seat like this:

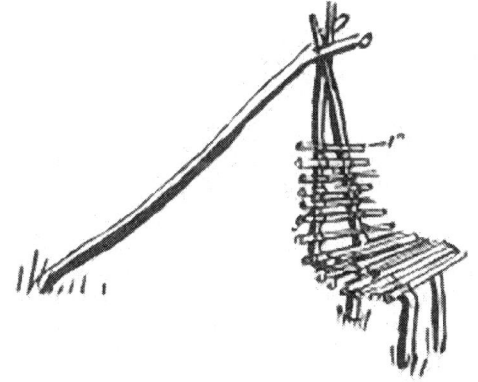

A good bushman makes himself comfortable wherever he may be. The simplest seat, of course, is either to roll up a log, or failing that, to select your site where a fallen tree will serve you. Such are not always to be found, and you can often make a comfortable seat by using a few stones to build up a platform, and between these you can lay two or three poles for your seat.

Camp Seat

A very comfortable fireside camp seat can be made by driving two short stakes into the ground, so that the forks are pointing outwards, that is, away from the opposite stake. The bottom of the forks should be from 8 to 10 inches above the ground level.

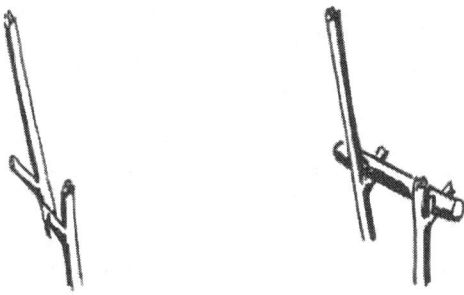

Two back forked stakes about three feet six inches long are driven into the ground, 15 to 18 inches behind these two short stakes. These back stakes should be driven in on a slight angle, leaning away from the two forward forks. The forks of the rear stakes should point outwards.

Both short and long stakes should be not less than two inches thick and the fork at least one and a half inches thick.

The short stakes should be at a convenient distance from the fireplace, anything from three feet to six feet, depending upon the size fire you usually build.

Cut two cross-bars, each about 3 inches thick, and cut nicks in these so they fit snugly in place in the forks, and connect front and rear forks.

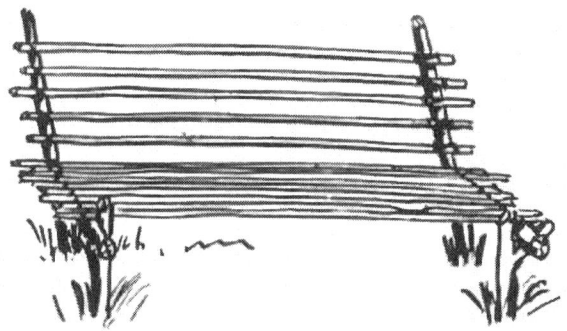

Lengthways, lay straight smooth sticks, one to two inches thick. These must be close together. Along the back, that is to the tall stakes, lash similar sticks from 2 to 3 inches apart.

This makes an excellent fireside camp seat, and the comfort it gives you will well repay the half-hour it took to build.

Camp Beds

A sound night's rest is worth ten minutes' toil. Time spent in making a camp bed that will keep you both comfortable and warm is time well spent.

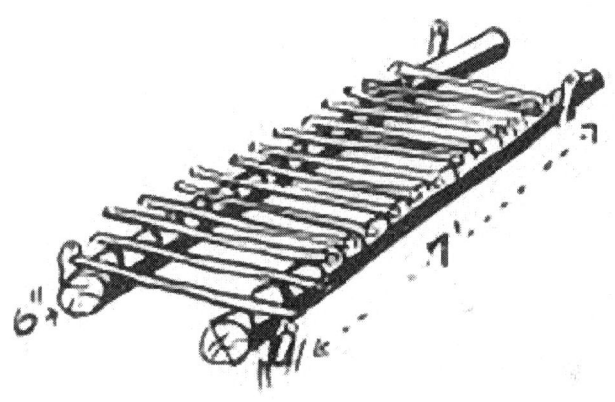

Cut two poles six or seven inches thick, and about seven feet long. Lay these parallel to each other, three feet apart; and to prevent them rolling, put pegs at head and foot, driven well into the ground with about a foot of the peg above the pole. Cut about twenty or thirty straight, strong sticks, three and a half feet long, and lay these every four inches across the two poles. Now on top of these cross sticks place two poles, three to four inches thick and seven feet long. They should lie against the pegs driven in to hold the two "bed" poles secure.

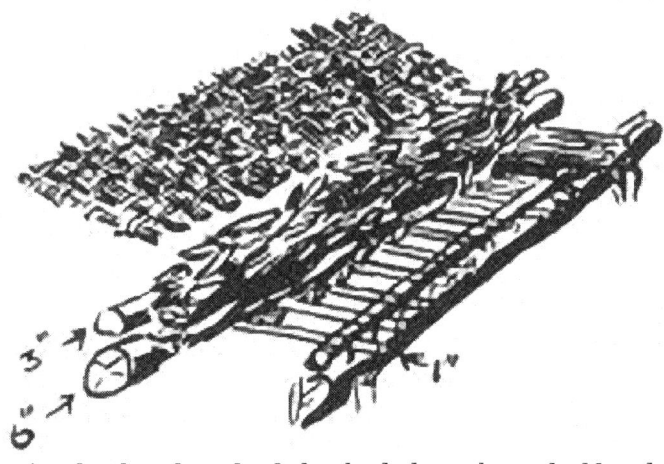

At the head end of the bed, lay about half a dozen cross sticks on top of these last two poles. Now cut green brushwood, fern, or waste green stuff, such as sucker growth, or weedy bush material, and put this so that the main stalks are lengthways along the bed. Pile it high between the two top poles, and lying across the cross sticks. The resulting bed will be as springy and comfortable as any you have ever slept on in your life.

If you are going to be in camp for a long period, you had better make yourself a camp mattress from grass on the camp loom, and if bedding is short you can weave a covering from dried grass on the same loom, and sleep as warm and snug as if you were between the blankets in your own bed at home.

Camp Bed Off the Ground

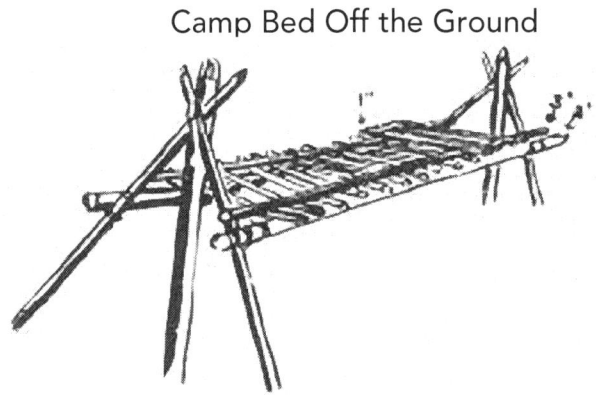

A framework, similar to the table, with the table top only, is made, and the two poles are overlaid with sticks exactly as for the bed on the ground. When making a bed off the ground it is not necessary to have the forks as high as for the table. A camp bed should always be built off the ground in bad snake country, or in areas where ground pests such as leeches, ants, scrub-mites, chiggers or ticks are liable to be troublesome.

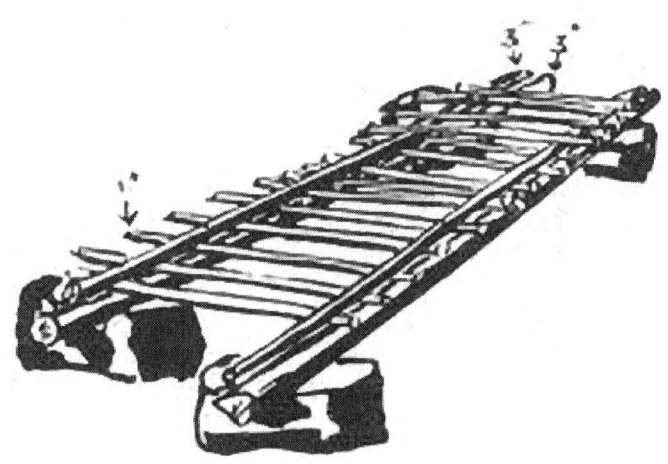

An alternative to the forked stakes and ground poles is the use of two piles of stones to support the sidepoles.

Camp Bed Using a Couple of Bags

A very comfortable camp bed can be made by setting up the two forked stakes as for the preceding camp bed, and two side poles are placed into the crotches of these so they are about 45 degrees slope. Two long, straight poles are cut, and passed through the two sides of two bags (holes are cut in the bottoms of each of the bags to allow the poles to pass through). The closed ends of the bags are towards the ends of the poles, and the bags overlap a few inches in the middle. The two bed poles with the bags are laid one on either side of the angle poles. The weight of the body, lying on the bags, keeps the side poles pulled well down on the angle poles. If the weather is cold, or greater comfort is required, a stuffing of dried grass or bracken fern inside the bags will serve to give greater softness, and also make this type of bed warmer.

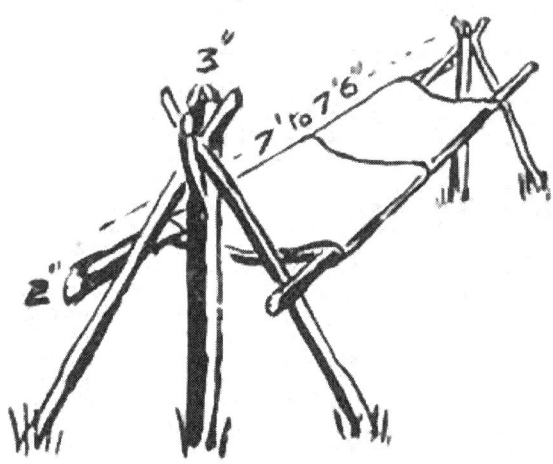

Stick Hammock

A camp loom is set up, and the hammock is woven, using vines, twisted bark fibres, grass rope or any suitable material for the weaving, and sticks about one inch thick for the cross parts. The hammock should be at least three feet wide by six feet six inches long. The end two spreaders should be two inches thick, and from these short lengths of rope are brought to the the hammock. A grass mattress, also woven on the camp loom, makes an excellent cover for the hammock.

Camp Loom

Two stout forked stakes, about two inches thick, are cut and driven into the ground with their lower prongs three feet above the ground, and facing away from the direction you wish to work. The distance between the stakes should be at least six inches wider than the widest article you want to weave. Across the forks a cross bar, about one inch thick, is laid. It is advisable to trim this cross bar of twigs and roughnesses. It should be fairly strong.

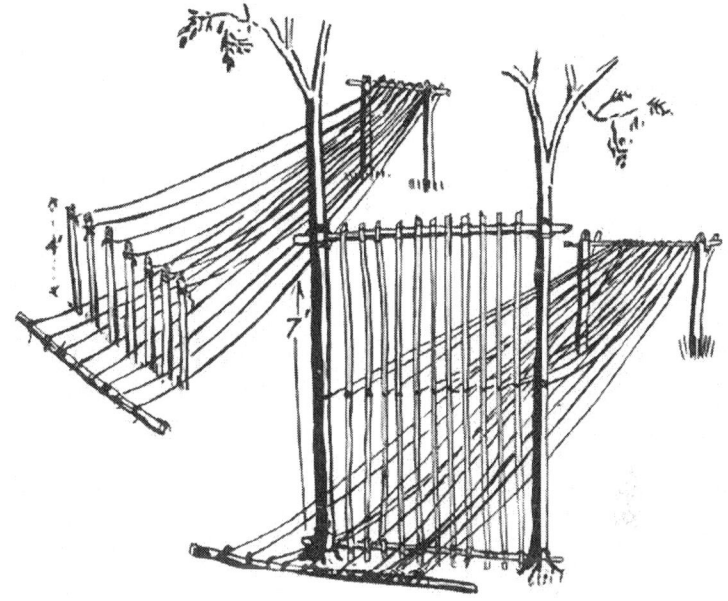

Eight or nine feet from the cross bar, and on the side farthest from the prongs, a row of straight, smooth stakes, each about four feet long, is driven into the ground so that there are about two inches between the centres of the stakes. These stakes should be trimmed of any side twigs or roughnesses. A weaving bar, a few inches longer than the width of the row of stakes, is cut and laid on the ground, parallel and about six inches in front of this row of stakes.

Your camp loom is now ready to be set up for weaving.

An alternative to the row of stakes, and a considerable improvement if a situation is available, is to select a site where two trees are at a convenient distance apart. At ground level, and about seven feet above the ground, two stout cross bars, two inches thick, are lashed to the tree trunks, and to these crossbars a series of smooth vertical sticks are lashed at top and bottom. These sticks are about two inches apart at centres.

To Weave on a Camp Loom

Lengths of the weaving material are tied to the stakes as shown, brought back over the cross bar, and then forward and between the stakes, and then tied to the weaving bar in front of the row of stakes. (This is the "weft" of your weaving.) A ball of material is tied to the outside strand, and then passed between the two rows of strands (this is the warp), with the weaving bar lying on the ground. The weaving bar is lifted above the weft, and the ball returned again between the weft threads. Repeat by alternately lifting and lowering the weaving bar.

Camp Mattress of Stick Hammock

The weft or long strands are set up as for weaving, but instead of warp (cross strands), tufts of grass, fern or other material (or sticks if for a stick hammock) are passed between the weft. In weaving a camp mattress it is advisable to put in a warp tie every second or third lift. This binds the sides and prevents the outside weft strands spreading.

Strands of sun-dried grass, loosely spun, can be woven into a covering for a camp bed if you are without blankets. When weaving for this purpose, make sure that the warp strands are pushed closely up to each other. Do not try and make a camp blanket too heavy. It is better to make two light grass coverings than one heavy one . . . it is a number of layers, rather than extreme thickness of one layer, which keeps you warm.

Weaving a Camp Hammock

Normally a hammock is made by using the netting tie, and netting needle (not shown in this book), but a serviceable hammock can be woven on the camp loom from bush materials. The ball of warp is passed around the weft threads to form an overhand knot on the lower lay of the weft, and these knots, pulled tight, make the weaving secure.

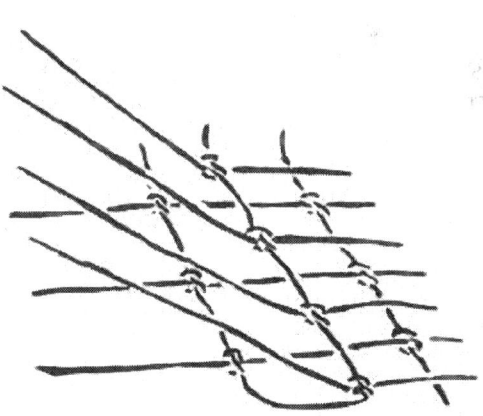

Bush Ladder

A bush ladder is easily made. Select two long, straight poles cut to equal length. Lash the thin ends together. Spread the butts or thick ends so that they are about two and a half to three feet apart. To these lash the rungs, and make certain that the lashings are good and tight. Lashing the rungs is made easier if you lift the butts on to a log or a couple of big stones. This will allow you to pass the lashing material more easily under the poles.

Single Rope Ladder

Cut as many hardwood chocks, 1½ to 2 inches thick, as you require for your ladder. These are placed every fifteen to eighteen inches apart. The chocks should be about four inches across and can be cut from either square or round timber. Bore a hole through the centre of each chock. This hole should not be more than one-eighth inch larger than the diameter of the rope.

Thread the rope through the holes in the chocks and then, starting at one end, open the strand of the rope and slip in a half-inch thick hardwood peg about three inches long. Bind the rope below the peg. Slide the chock down, and measure off the distance to the next step. If desired, bind above the chock to prevent the feet pulling it up when climbing.

If using braided cotton rope omit

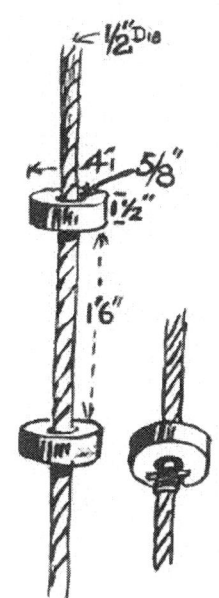

Swinging Shelter

A forked pole, at least four to five inches thick, and eight feet long, with a side branch coming off at right angles to the fork and four to five feet below it, is required. To the side branch a rope or very strong vine loop is secured, passed around a tree trunk, and then bound very securely back on to the side branch. The long arm of the pole should be horizontal and six to seven feet above the ground.

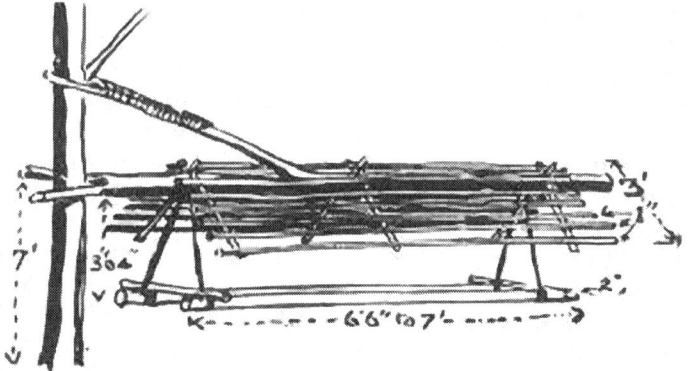

To make the shelter top, lash three 3-ft. stakes, each about 2 inches thick, to each side of the pole. They should slope down at an angle of about forty-five degrees, and can be held outwards by lashing braces across.

Lengthways to these poles lash thatching battens, each about 1 inch thick and eight feet long. These should be six inches apart. They are then thatched with grass, fern palms or reeds. (Branches and tree leaves are useless.)

The bed is suspended from the centre pole by ropes or vines to the two long sides, which are held apart by lashing two cross-bars at head and foot. The bed is then made up like the camp bed.

This shelter can be swung round the tree trunk to take advantage of sun or shade or get better protection from the weather.

Slush Lamp

A lamp for your camp is made by filling an old tin or small hollow piece of branch with clayey earth, packed tight at the bottom. The earth should come to about an inch from the top of the tin. Into this a twig is pushed and a piece of old cotton rag, or very finely teased bark fibre, is wound round the twig to serve as a wick. Fat from your cooking is poured on top of the earth, and when the wick is lit the lamp burns with a clear flame. The amount of light can be controlled by the size of wick.

A Candle Holder From a Bottle

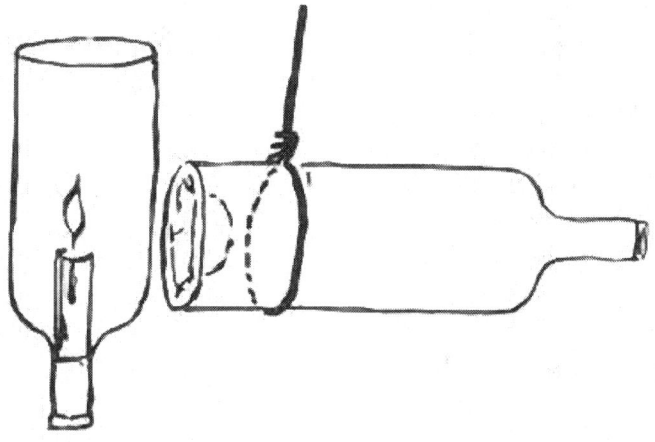

An open flame in a tent is dangerous, and a candle holder or glass cover for a slush lamp can be made by cutting off the base of a clear glass bottle. A very easy way to cut the glass cleanly is to heat a piece of thin wire to red heat. Bend this around the bottle where you want to cut it (alternatively, tie a piece of grease-soaked string round the bottle and burn it), and then, when the hot wire or burning string is around the bottle, immerse the bottle in cold water. The glass will break off evenly at the place where the wire or string encircled it.

Noggin

On many trees you will see lumpy growths or "burls", varying in size from a few inches to a foot or more. These are covered completely over with bark, and if you examine one closely you will find that under the bark the wood is all solid, and the growth is complete, without any holes where branches might have once grown.

Cut off the lump by making a scarf an inch or so above and another below the growth. A side-cut with your axe will then slice the wood with the burl completely free. Roughly trim the surplus wood, and with a gouge clean out the wood from the centre of the burl. This is very easy, because the grain follows the curves of the growth. Leave a handle in the form of a lip, and if you so wish, bore a hole through this handle and put a leather loop through the hole. A coconut shell makes an excellent noggin.

Clothes Pegs

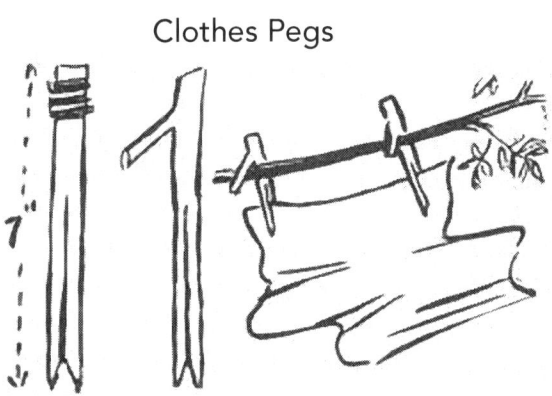

Clothes pegs are quickly made by taking a number of half-green sticks, about seven inches long, and splitting them, first binding the end so that they will not split right along their length. A better way is to use a forked stick, hooking the hook part on to a branch.

Camp Broom

A bundle of green straight sticks, each not much thicker than a matchstick, is collected and bound tightly to a central handle. The business end of the broom is then trimmed off.

Bush Hoe

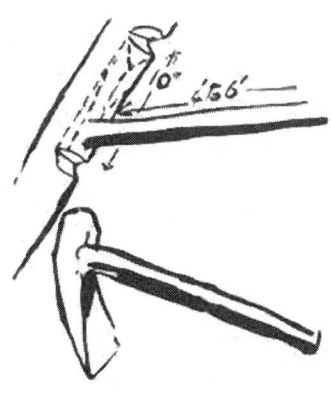

Select a dead or half-dead branch of hardwood, four to six inches thick, with a side branch from five to six feet long and an inch and a half thick coming off it at a fairly wide angle. Trim the side branch so that it is smooth. With your machete or tomahawk, trim the main branch so that it is a "hook" to the handle part. See that it is sharpened to a chisel edge. This bush hoe is quite an efficient digging tool, particularly if the digging end is fire hardened.

Bush Sled

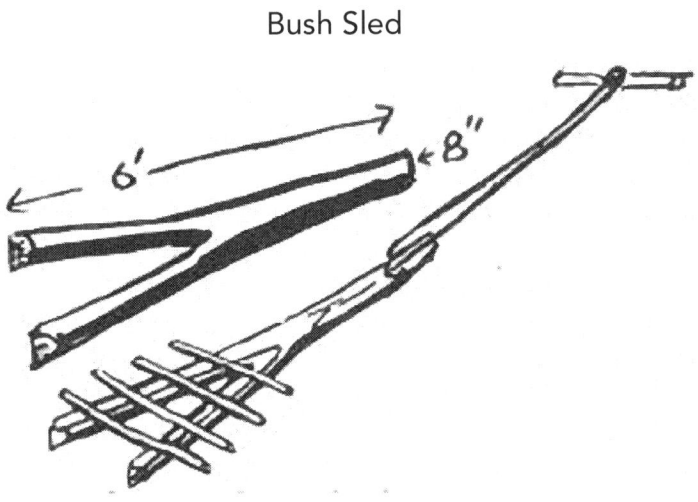

There are occasions when it is necessary to move a heavy load, and for this purpose a bush sled can be easily made from a forked branch of a tree. The branch is cut with the prongs of the fork a couple of feet behind the end of the main branch. A rope or other means of towing the sled is fastened on to this main part of the branch, and across the forks a few straight sticks are laid, and the load placed on top of these.

Camp Larder

A camp larder is simply a platform, roofed over with thatch and with the sides thatched so that it is dark and cool inside. Darkness will help to keep flies away, and coolness will help to prevent food going bad. An excellent improvement to a camp larder is a water tin suspended above the thatch, with a few pieces of cotton rag to siphon water on to a thatched roof. This is almost a camp refrigerator. The temperature inside such a larder, if built in a shady position and with a good breeze, will be easily twenty to forty degrees below the shade temperature outside.

Other methods of storing food in camp away from animals include placing it in a hollow log wedged in the crotch of a tree, or suspending it from a bough, or making a platform and suspending this from a branch in a shady position. If ants are a pest, suspending the platform is probably one of the best ways to keep them away from your food. If they do find the cord, you can prevent them from travelling along to your food by tying a kerosene-soaked rag around the cord. Another method is to break a bottle off above the neck, pass the cord through the cork, and then, after packing clay around the rope where it passes the neck, fill with water. Water will soak down the rope and the bottle will need frequent filling.

Camp Coat Hanger

Usually in camp, one's travelling clothes become crushed and soiled. This can easily be prevented by making a simple coat and trousers hanger. If you take off your good clothes immediately you arrive in camp and put them on this coat-hanger, they will remain fresh and uncreased.

Camp Pack Frame

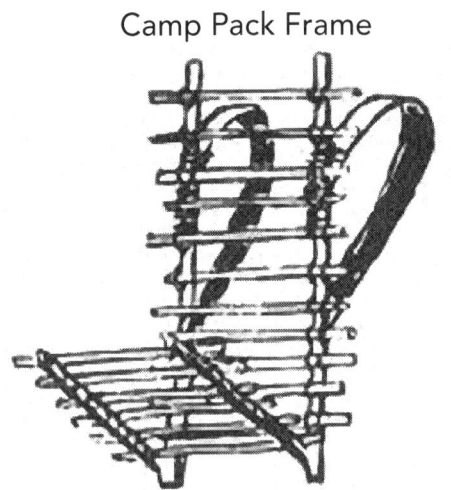

This "Adirondack" pack frame is a good method of carrying gear in camp. The cross sticks are tightly lashed to the two hooked sticks. Shoulder straps are plaited from reeds or made from wide strips of soft bark.

Camp Sun Clock

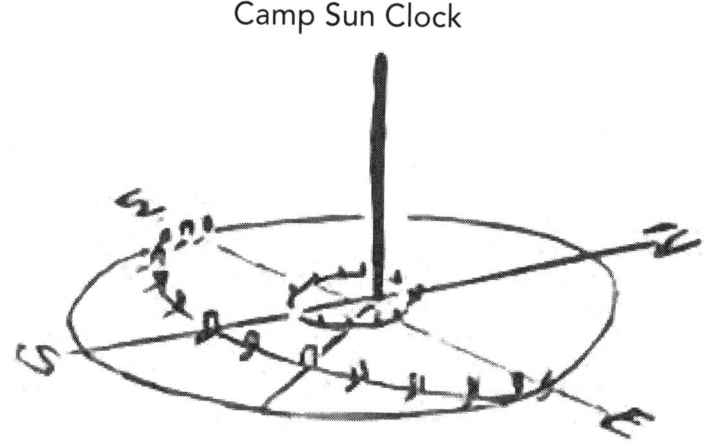

Select a patch of bare earth near your camp. It must be level, and open to the sun all day. Stick a peg in the centre of this patch, and with a length of cord as a loop around the peg, scratch a circle on the ground. This must be at least five feet across. From the peg, which is now the centre of the circle, carefully draw a line TRUE north. This must be accurately TRUE, and not Magnetic. Extend this line to cut the southern side of the circle, and then draw in accurate East-West lines crossing at the circle's centre.

Divide the circumference of the circle into twenty-four equal divisions. Each of these divisions will be fifteen degrees.

Now have a look at your map and find out what degree of latitude you are in. Measure this in degrees on the out side circle, working from where it is cutting the East-West line. Put a small peg on each side of the circle's edge to mark the latitude degrees.

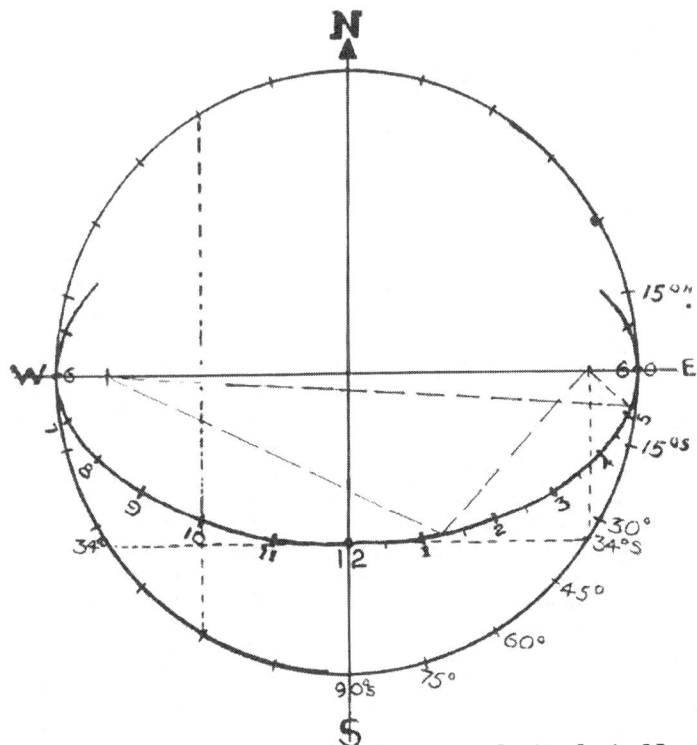

Be careful to note whether your latitude is North or South of the Equator. Stretch the cord over the two pegs and mark where it crosses the North-South line. Now put a peg on the North-South line where the cord crosses it. Next, put two other pegs at either end of the East-West line so that the "degree" pegs on the circle are at right angles. Tie a cord to each of these pegs, and have the cord pass round the peg on the North-South line. Lift the cord over the centre peg, and with the point of your knife, scratch an elipse on the ground, so that it touches the circle where the East-West line crosses, and also touches the point on the North-South line where the peg is.

Connect up the fifteen degree marks on the circle by means of the cord and parallel with the North-South line. Where the cord crosses the ellipse, put a small peg very firmly into the ground.

There will be thirteen of these pegs, and they will follow the curve of the ellipse. These are the hour pegs, starting from 6 a.m. on the left, where the West line cuts the circle, 12 noon on the North-South line, and 6 p.m. on the right where the East line cuts the circle.

You must now know how to find where to place the shadow stick. This depends on the sun's position North or South of the Equator.

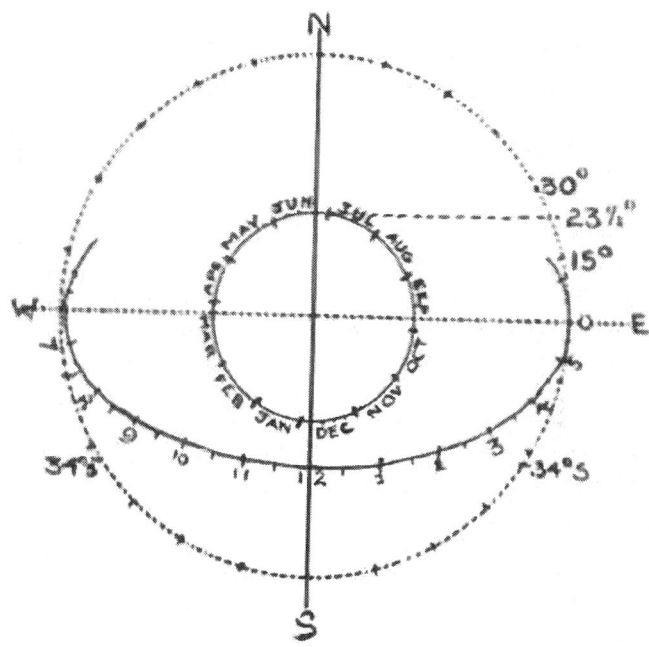

To Find the Sun's Position North or South of the Equator

Draw another circle inside the big circle using the same centre. The radius of this circle must be equal to 23½ degrees of the big circle. Divide this circle into twelve equal divisions and mark June at the North side; July, etc., follow clockwise. Divide June into four equal divisions, and do the same with December (at the South end). Offset ALL divisions one-fourth in a clockwise direction. The North-South line will now pass through the third division of June and December. Put pegs in for each of the twelve months' divisions.

To find the sun's position at any time of the year, draw a line from the month, and approximate day thereof, to the North-South line. This must parallel the East-West line. Where this line cuts the North-South line is where you place your shadow stick.

To get absolutely reliable time from the sun, two corrections for longitude, and for the "equation of time" are required.

The "shadow" reading, with these corrections, will be right to two minutes, if your North-South line has been accurate.

If West of the Meridian of Standard Time, add four minutes to sun clock time for each degree. East, deduct four minutes for each degree.

Draw a figure 8 near the sun clock on the ground, with the top half of the 8 just less than one-third the bottom half. Divide a line across the bottom half into three equal divisions on each side of a centre line.

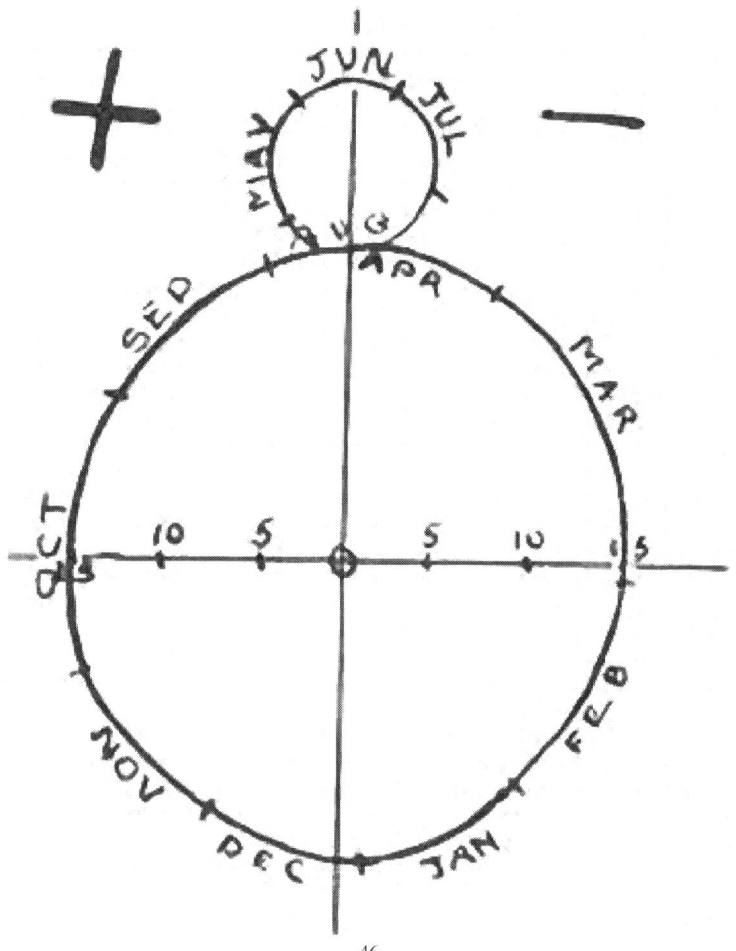

Each of these divisions represents five minutes of time. Now mark off the figure 8 into approximate divisions like the sketch. Put pegs in the ground to mark these divisions, and also the five minute divisions on the cross line.

Put a MINUS sign on the right-hand corner, and a plus on the right.

MINUS means that the sun time is behind clock time, and so you must ADD. Plus means that the sun time is ahead of clock time.

Made in the USA
Monee, IL
02 November 2019